AN

AUSTRIAN DIPLOMATIST

IN

THE FIFTIES

AN

AUSTRIAN DIPLOMATIST

IN

THE FIFTIES

*THE REDE LECTURE
DELIVERED IN THE CAMBRIDGE SENATE-HOUSE
ON JUNE 13, 1908*

BY

THE RIGHT HON. SIR ERNEST SATOW, G.C.M.G.

CAMBRIDGE :
AT THE UNIVERSITY PRESS
1908

CAMBRIDGE
UNIVERSITY PRESS

32 Avenue of the Americas, New York NY 10013-2473, USA

Cambridge University Press is part of the University of Cambridge.

It furthers the University's mission by disseminating knowledge in the pursuit of education, learning and research at the highest international levels of excellence.

www.cambridge.org
Information on this title: www.cambridge.org/9781107418851

First published 1908
First paperback edition 2014

A catalogue record for this publication is available from the British Library

ISBN 978-1-107-41885-1 Paperback

AN AUSTRIAN DIPLOMATIST
IN THE FIFTIES.

I T would naturally be expected of me that, in response to the invitation to lecture before this learned University, I should say something concerning events in which I have myself taken part during the many years of my life that have been spent abroad. Officers of the army and navy and Indian civilians on their retirement find their tongues untied. It is not so with Foreign Office agents. They are inhibited from publicly discussing the countries where they have served or narrating their own experiences, unless they have obtained the previous approval of the Secretary of State. This is a salutary rule, and one which I trust always to observe. Accordingly, I must, if I wish to speak of international affairs, go back to a period earlier than my own entrance into public life, and betake myself to a country where I have never served.

I have therefore chosen for my subject transactions which, for the most part, took place more than fifty years ago, in a capital with which I have had no official connexion.

In recent years the public has derived no small amount of entertainment, and the student of contemporary history much interesting information, from the publication of the memoirs of distinguished personages. Prince Bismarck's *Reflections and Reminiscences*, in which he claimed the credit of having so edited a comparatively harmless telegram as to bring about the war of 1870, form a marked example, and not long ago the hasty manner in which the memoirs of Prince Hohenlohe were launched forth, created wrathful excitement and even consternation in high places. It will be remembered what annoyance was caused some years earlier by the publication of La Marmora's *Un po' più di luce*, in which the genesis of the Prusso-Italian alliance of 1866 was exposed to the light of day. Minor instances of regrettable indiscretion have been plentiful, and I need not specify them. Old age loves to indulge itself in recalling the past, and the favourite amusement of the retired statesman is to write his reminiscences. As a rule he would do better not to publish them. If, in the interests of historical knowledge, it is desirable that the inner secrets of diplomacy should be unveiled, prudence would suggest a measure of delay, at least until the political events related have become so completely a portion of the past that no harm can result from the facts being disclosed. The death of the author is not sufficient justification for his posthumous tongue being immediately unloosed. It is difficult to excuse the publication of Guizot's memoirs, or of the correspondence of Palmerston, which relate the part they respectively played in the Spanish Marriages, when but a short time had elapsed since the accomplishment of that disastrous intrigue. A couple of centuries would perhaps not be too long a time to withhold the political papers of a Frederick the Great, while the diaries of a Busch and the piquant letters of a Sir Robert Morier to his Constantinople colleague might be kept back for no more than fifty. In England we are perhaps somewhat too indifferent to the revelation of political secrets. Sometimes more is communicated to Parliament and the public than is necessary, though Parliamentary papers often present gaps in the correspondence, and the more important documents seldom see the light. Nothing is to be gained by taking the world prematurely into the confidence of governments in regard to matters of high policy.

From the censure that, from this point of view, must be passed on most contemporary political memoirs, those of Hübner must be exempted. His first book, in which he related his share in the events of 1848–9, saw the light in 1891, and the more extensive journals of his ten years' residence in Paris as Austrian representative were published only in 1904, after his death, when most of his contemporaries had passed away. No fault can be found with him for setting down anything in malice, or any fact or opinion which could redound to the discredit of the government which he served with such skill, insight and devoted loyalty. It is true that he criticises freely the character and conduct of Napoleon III and his ministers. The dynasty of the Bonapartes has long passed away, and to judge from present signs there is no likelihood of its restoration. But he utters nothing injurious to the character of the French nation, nor anything calculated to diminish our admiration for a people inspired by an ardent love of liberty, by patriotism and the constant pursuit of the ideal in politics.

Since Sir Henry Wotton perpetrated for the

amusement of his Augsburg friend the well-known witticism which is popularly believed to describe the conduct characteristic of international agents, the general view has been that the weapons of the diplomatist are concealment, artifice, evasion, and systematic falsehood. It is curious to see what has been said of the diplomatic calling by those who do not belong to it. In M. Ollivier's *Empire Libérale* some very unfriendly opinions are quoted. Guizot, he says, complains that diplomacy abounds in proceedings and talk of no value, which can be neither ignored nor believed. Tocqueville is severe on the poor literary style of diplomatic correspondence. Cavour finds that diplomatists complicate questions instead of discovering their solution. Bismarck, writing to his wife, denounces the diplomacy pursued at Frankfort for its emptiness and charlatanism. M. Ollivier himself is even more severe. "I have been struck," he says, "with the constant uncertainty of the information given in the numerous

French, as well as foreign, diplomatic despatches I have read." He asserts that "in
spite of their theory that in public business
what is said differs from what the speaker really
thinks, even professional diplomatists end by let-
ting themselves be taken in like any ordinary
simpleton by the conventional tricks which they
practise on each other, and while fancying themselves clever, often fall into traps." He ex-
presses his surprise at finding how incapable
they are of forming an accurate judgment.
Nearly all of them are what Napoleon used to
call *ambassadeurs à conversations*, who make
it their business to repeat in detail their conversations with ministers and sovereigns, but
avoid compromising themselves by giving a decided opinion on what is said on such occasions.
They beat about the bush, they tack hither
and thither, envelope themselves in a cloud of
empty phrases, or still worse, they adopt the ex-
pedient of expressing one view in one part, and
an opposite one in another part of a despatch.

They are entirely engrossed by the particular question that has been entrusted to them, neglecting to take into account its proper place in the general scheme of policy: they magnify its importance, at the risk of hindering or compromising the more important action of their government in some other quarter. They allow themselves to convert business discussions into personal matters, are sensitive to small slights, somebody has not bowed low enough to them, they have been kept waiting for a decoration they expected, their wives have not been treated with due respect; they occupy their minds less with their negotiations than with the satisfaction of their spite, or rather they regard its satisfaction as the success of their negotiation. He finds among the diplomatists of the Second Empire "busy-bodies on the look-out for sensational news, scatter-brains who perceived nothing of the events passing around them and heard nothing of the conversations which took place in their presence, self-important asses, presumptuous persons who imagine themselves to have predicted everything that happened, trying to demonstrate all this in their dull correspondence, egotists whose only care was to render themselves *persona grata* to the government to which they were accredited, forgetting that the triumph of a really patriotic diplomatist consists the rather in being disliked by those whose schemes he has to watch, expose and thwart."

This, if well-founded, is a serious indictment, and would go far to justify those who have proposed to abolish the diplomatic profession altogether. It is fair, however, to listen to the other side. The first requisite of the historian, it has been acutely said, is kindliness, and if it is too much to ask from a critic that he should treat his victim as if he loved him, it is certain that no judgment can be sound that is not informed by sympathy. From an eloquent lawyer and leader of advanced radicals what amount of this could be expected for a calling that is naturally of a conservative temper, and whose motto should be *il viso sciolto ed i pensieri stretti.*

Let Hübner speak for his cloth. He exclaims : "What a trying profession is that of the diplomatist. I know of none which demands so much self-denial, so much readiness to sacrifice interest to duty, so much patience and at times so much courage. The ambassador who fulfils the duties of his office never betrays fatigue, boredom nor disgust. He keeps to himself the emotions he experiences, the temptations to weakness that assail him. He has to remain silent regarding the bitter disappointments to which he is subjected, as well as the unexpected successes which chance sometimes, but rarely, bestows on him. While jealous of his own dignity, he is constantly mindful of others, is careful not to fall out with any one, never loses his serenity, and in great crises, when it is a question of peace or war, shows himself calm, unmoved and confident of success."

It is certain that during all the period in which Hübner played such an important part in the development of European history, he, at least, lived and acted in accordance with this lofty ideal. Perhaps it would be safe to say that every nation has the diplomatists which it deserves.

The hero of my discourse entered the Austrian service in 1833 at the age of twenty-two, and after serving abroad at various posts, was summoned to Vienna by Prince Metternich in February, 1848. The state of Italy, where a fire had been smouldering under the ashes for several months, required the presence at Milan of an experienced diplomatist as adviser to the Archduke Rainier, and to keep up constant communication with the Italian governments. For this responsible task he had been chosen by the great chancellor. After Radetzky's retreat on Verona, he made his way back to Vienna, where he was employed in various missions and negotiations with leading political personages, while his practised pen was utilized in the preparation of the most important state-papers of the period.   A confidential position of this class had familiarized Hübner with the policy of the Austrian government.   Whilst firmly insisting on the treaties of 1815 and on the maintenance of their territorial rights and political influence in Italy, the Austrian government were willing to act in concert with France for the restoration of the Temporal Power.   To this end a friendly understanding was necessary with Louis-Napoleon, who must, if possible, be detached from Palmerston— that notorious sympathizer with Italian revo-lutionists—and be encouraged to regard himself as the saviour of society in France.   Cir-cumstances pointed to Hübner as the most fitting agent for the purpose, and in March, 1849, he was accordingly despatched to Paris.   His efforts were to be directed towards keeping the Prince-President in an attitude of neutrality, and he was to employ all the means which circumstances or his own reflections might suggest. Schwarzenberg's words of farewell were : "I count on you, and you can count on me. I have never left anyone in the lurch."

The hope that he might persuade Louis-Napoleon to remain neutral was only partly fulfilled. A momentary tension between the two governments had been produced by the battle of Novara, and France seemed on the point of declaring war. Fortunately Hübner received timely information. With the help of the leaders of the Assembly, and especially of Thiers, he succeeded in dissuading the President from taking the decisive step which would have brought on hostilities. At the same time he warned Schwarzenberg of the danger, and peace was promptly signed with Piedmont. Austria having the civil war in Hungary on her hands was in no position to lightly incur the risk of war with France, any more than she could have ventured to oppose the French expedition to Rome.

Hübner's *Souvenirs d'un Ambassadeur*

include three events of first-rate importance, the
coup d'état of 2nd December, 1851, followed a
year later by the proclamation of the Empire,
the Crimean War, and the outbreak of the war
for the liberation of Italy.

In discussing the first of these he remarks
that for twenty years past Louis-Napoleon had
dreamed of ascending the throne of his uncle.
He describes him as a restless spirit, dreamy
and flighty ; his schemes for a constitution and
for legislation were all coloured by imperialist
traditions and revolutionary doctrines picked up
among the secret societies of which he had been
and still was a member ; yet, with all that, he
was not entirely devoid of conservative instincts.
That explained, according to Hübner, the per-
plexed and hesitating frame of mind ascribed to
him by his immediate intimates.   It was said
that at times he dreamt of nothing but war and
conquest.   He would be a second Napoleon I.
At other times he cherished the idea of a peace-
ful reign passed in all manner of gratification.

But, for this the *sine quâ non* would be a conservative policy calculated to re-assure the older crowned heads, and to induce them to admit him into their ranks. To be sure, being, as a Bonapartist and a Carbonaro, doubly a child of the revolution, in his case a military conspiracy could never become the foundation of a monarchy. He might nevertheless possibly be kept from kicking over the traces, for a time at least, if not for the whole of his reign. To the task, therefore, of convincing Louis-Napoleon that it would be to his interest to inspire Europe with confidence, to let the irregular and alarming manner in which he had attained power be forgotten, and with this object to endow France with institutions of as conservative a character as possible, Hübner addressed himself. He was willing, like the faithful disciple of Metternich that he was, to regard Louis-Napoleon as the instrument appointed by Providence to deal a mortal blow to parliamentary institutions on the continent.

In another place he describes the President as full of craft and possessing all the arts of a conspirator, but entirely deficient in practical ability, in aptitude for well-conceived schemes, in the skill requisite for their execution, and in the virtues and qualities of a leader of men. Louis-Napoleon's strength lay in his disbelief in the "phantom of parliamentarism, in which all French politicians since 1814 had put their faith." After another year's intercourse he styles him a mixture of contradictions, both cunning and simple-minded, a rake and an idealist, addicted to pleasure, and a lover of the marvellous, sometimes sincere, systematically impenetrable when he liked, always conspiring, as much for the love of the thing as from habit, and always—in good or evil fortune—a fatalist believing in his star.

Schwarzenberg's death in April, 1852, was a great blow to Hübner, who lost in him his most powerful political friend and patron, to whom he could always speak his opinion with perfect frankness, and who often acted on his advice. The new chancellor was Buol, a former colleague, of whose capacity Hübner had no very exalted opinion. In one place he says: " I know his weak points, but I appreciate his good qualities. He is not a statesman of the highest class, but a diplomatist of a good school, intelligent when passion does not cloud his judgment: often, too often, disagreeable, but at bottom kind, honourable and loyal." One of Buol's weak points certainly was bad temper, which is a serious defect in a foreign minister. His policy for the moment was to prevent, or at least retard, the establishment of the Empire, and to this end he used to furnish Hübner with all manner of arguments, good, bad and indifferent, which the latter had to repeat till he was sick of them, and, as it proved altogether fruitlessly, to the Prince and his advisers.

It is a question, I think, whether in political matters it is wise to fight against a foregone conclusion, instead of accepting it with a good grace and making the best of a bad job. The language which to Buol in his study at Vienna seemed so calculated to convince would probably have appeared to him futile if he had been ambassador at Paris. For Austria at least, considering her position in Italy, Louis-Napoleon's notorious sympathies with Italian aspirations towards liberty and independence, and the secular rivalry between France and Austria in Italian politics, it might have been wiser to acquiesce in the inevitable.

Yet it seems that the attitude of the Powers made Louis-Napoleon hesitate about assuming the title of Emperor. Before finally making up his mind he sounded the three Northern Courts. At Vienna and Berlin he met with little encouragement, while at Petersburg he found very strong opposition. Nicholas I not only forbade his officials to take any notice of the *fête Napoléon*, but also persuaded the Emperor of Austria and the King of Prussia to give similar instructions. It was after this that Louis-

Napoleon said in a speech at Bordeaux : "France appears to desire to return to the Empire. In a spirit of mistrust certain people say 'the Empire means war': I say 'the Empire means peace.'" This utterance was often thrown in his teeth afterwards.

The die was now cast. On November 4th the Senate was convoked to listen to a message from the Prince-President, and on the 7th it presented a Senatus-consultum, re-establishing the Empire in his person and conferring on him power to nominate his successors in default of a direct heir. A few days later Hübner received despatches from Vienna, from which he learnt that great irritation was felt by the three Courts, all the greater because it was perfectly well understood that nothing could be done in the way of prevention. This explained to him the moderate tone of Buol's official despatches and the strong language of his private letters. The position of Hübner and his Russian and Prussian colleagues was no easy one. If they conducted

themselves prudently they would be charged
with lukewarmness or timidity, but if they took
an opposite line they ran the risk of involving
their governments in complications with France.
In England the disposition of the government
was conciliatory, and Cowley told him that the
title Napoleon III, which was the great
stumbling-stone of the three Northern Courts,
would not encounter any objection. On
November 21, at a ball at the Tuileries, Hübner
had over an hour's conversation with Louis-
Napoleon, who himself alluded to the difficulties
attaching to the figure III, and they discussed
the very delicate question of recognition.
Hübner spoke very frankly, and Louis-Napoleon
listened attentively, but without allowing that
he was convinced. Two days later came fresh
instructions from Buol, characterized by a provoking ambiguity. The official despatches
preserved a tone of moderation, but the private
letter breathed fire and fury. That was nothing
in comparison with the orders from Berlin, con-

fused, contradictory, expressing anger mingled
with fear, which poured down like a flood on his
unlucky colleague Hatzfeld. On December 1
the legislature proceeded to Saint-Cloud to
report the result of the plebiscite, 7,800,000
affirmative votes. Louis-Napoleon had become
a Majesty, Emperor, and Napoleon III. For
the man in the street and for the ordinary
courtier, says Hübner, the recognition of the
Empire must have appeared a mere question of
etiquette. Statesmen, who are never very plentiful, as he remarks, knew that war and peace
depended on the course which the Great Powers
would adopt.

An occasion of friction had already arisen
between the Emperor Nicholas and Louis-
Napoleon in 1849, in connexion with the demand
made upon the Porte by Austria and Russia for
the extradition of Kossuth and other Hungarian
patriots. This had left a sore behind. What
was more serious was, that by the treaty of
11 April, 1814, Napoleon I had renounced the

throne of France for himself and all members of
his family.   During the thirty-seven years that
had elapsed since 1815 the provisions of the
" Acte du congrès de Vienne " had been departed
from in more than one instance, and other things
had happened which it might be argued were
infringements of the treaties concluded at that
period.   It is a doctrine of international law
that a treaty provision can only be annulled
by the common consent of those who were
parties to it, but in practice it is not always
observed, least of all when it can only be
insisted on at the risk of war.   The three Powers
were not prepared to use force to prevent Louis-
Napoleon from assuming the title of Emperor.
The cypher III implied heredity of the throne
in the Bonaparte family.   Nicholas I cordially
detested sovereigns whose title was derived from
a revolution.   He had refused to Louis-Philippe
the address of " Monsieur mon frère," and had
as far as possible ignored his existence.   He
could be relied on to join in administering a

snub to Napoleon III. Buol accordingly proposed to Petersburg and Berlin that while
recognizing the Empire, the credentials of their
diplomatic representatives should begin simply
with "Sire." The Emperor of Russia thought
this too stiff, and suggested the addition of *et
bon ami*, which was accepted, at least at Vienna.
Then the King of Prussia, unwilling to offend
the new Power, decided after all to adopt the
usual formula. Buol, not venturing to be less
cordial, followed suit. As Hübner observes,
Russia had not France for a neighbour on the
Rhine, nor had she a Lombardo-Venetian
kingdom to cause her anxiety. Instructions
were nevertheless sent to the three ministers to
act in concert, which was impracticable, as their
governments were not in agreement. They
were also to make "reserves" in regard to the
cypher III, and to his being succeeded by any
other member of his family, which amounted to
nothing more than a demonstration of ill-will.
In order to preserve the show of united action,

the three diplomatists agreed that Hübner and Hatzfeld should not present their credentials unless those of Kisseleff, in which the obnoxious formula was preserved, were also accepted. Drouyn de Lhuys and Persigny did their best to persuade Louis-Napoleon to refuse their reception, and he was about to publish a declaration of his reasons for taking this course, when Morny at the last moment prevailed on him to adopt the wiser and more prudent line of action. The Russian minister accordingly had his audience on the 5th January. M. Ollivier relates how Napoleon III took his revenge. Instead of passing the credentials, in the usual manner, to his Minister for Foreign Affairs, he broke the seal himself, read the letter deliberately, and then said to the ambassador : "You will thank His Imperial Majesty warmly for his kindness, and above all for the expression 'good friend' of which he has made use, for one has to endure one's brothers, and one chooses one's friends." To mark his displeasure at the

pressure that had been put on him to submit
to this affront, he postponed the audiences of
the Austrian and Prussian representatives for a
whole week. The diplomatists breathed again,
but it can hardly be doubted that the offence
rankled in the Emperor's bosom, and had a
large share in provoking his subsequent action
in support of Turkey and in bringing about the
Crimean War. This, at least, was Hübner's
opinion, expressed over and over again. The
complaisance of Austria in regard to the formula
of address was not placed to her credit, and did
not help her to retain Lombardy when the time
came for the consideration of the Italian
question.

In the excitement of the crisis the small
cloud in the East had escaped notice. This was
what is known as the affair of the Holy Places.
It was started by General Lahitte, the incom-
petent Minister for Foreign Affairs in Louis-
Napoleon's cabinet of July, 1849, at the in-
stigation of Montalembert. La Valette, who had

just arrived in Constantinople as ambassador, saw in it an opportunity of gaining credit for himself. As Hübner observes, the gravity of the complications which might result was entirely ignored by the politicians who initiated the diplomatic campaign. Lahitte was succeeded by Turgot, more ignorant, if possible, of politics than his predecessor. By dint of threats, concessions were extorted from the Porte which it could not grant without violating previous engagements with Russia. In this manner the Eastern question was needlessly revived, and the dangerous character of these incidents was lost sight of even at Vienna.

For Hübner the Italian question was a perpetual nightmare. He had been sent to Paris to restrain Louis-Napoleon from adopting an active policy in Italian affairs and disturbing the *status quo* in that peninsula. As a follower of Metternich he naturally mistrusted Russia, and was the vigorous advocate of a policy directed towards bringing Austria into line with the two Western Powers against her. His principal difficulties lay in the pro-Russian sympathies of the Emperor Francis-Joseph's military advisers and the vacillating character of his immediate chief Buol. He had to proceed with caution, as every diplomatist must who wishes to convert his government to what he believes to be the right policy. It was necessary to persuade the Austrian Court to evince a more friendly disposition than it had shown in connexion with the recognition of the Second Empire, and to depart from the bullying attitude towards Turkey they had taken up in the affair of the Hungarian refugees. In the latter he was not at first successful. Montenegro having refused to pay tribute and allowed raids to take place into Turkish territory, Omar Pasha proceeded to occupy the Principality. On this Austria despatched an ultimatum in January, 1853, demanding instant evacuation. The Porte gave way with unexpected readiness, and thus terminated satisfactorily an incident which

Hübner regarded as diametrically opposed to the traditional Austrian policy, namely to treat the sick man gently, and try to keep the breath in his body rather than to administer blows that might ruin his constitution and produce a collapse. The secret was that Nicholas I, by supporting the Austrian demands, had given the Turks grounds for suspecting that he would shortly apply the same procedure for his own ends, and hence the facility with which they had yielded to Austria. However this may be, the original dispute about the Holy Places having been arranged through the intervention of Stratford de Redcliffe, further demands were presented by Russia. Their acceptance would have established a Russian protectorate over some ten millions of the Sultan's subjects in Europe. Their refusal was followed by the withdrawal of the Menschikoff mission, and the entry of Russian troops into the Principalities. After some ineffectual negotiations at Constantinople and Vienna, with the object of reconciling the rights of the Porte and the dignity of the Emperor Nicholas, the Turks came to an end of their patience, announced that the continuance of peace would depend on the evacuation of the Principalities within a fortnight, and finally commenced hostilities against the Russian forces on the Danube, on the last day of October, 1853.

Already in June Hübner had given Buol an indication of what the future was likely to bring forth. Drouyn de Lhuys, he repeated, was telling everyone that if England and France joined in the fray Austria would be unable to stand aloof, and again in September he wrote in the same strain. Finally, in a private letter written a fortnight after hostilities had begun, he demonstrated to his chief that if the two Western Powers went to war with Russia, it would be impossible for Austria to remain neutral.

This letter produced a complete change of tone at Vienna, and affords the key to the subsequent conduct of Austria. It became recognized that France could injure her far more by a hostile policy in Italy than could Russia on the Danube, hampered as the latter would be by a war with England and France. The alliance to which the three powers ultimately became parties in December, 1854, and the corresponding convention between Austria and France, stipulating that no alteration of a political or territorial nature should be permitted in Italy until the war was over, were the direct outcome of Hübner's appreciation of the situation. Throughout the Crimean War and at every phase of the negotiations which proceeded at Vienna he was never weary of preaching the necessity of joint action of some sort with the Western Powers and the danger of remaining neutral.

A curious incident, not, as far as I know, mentioned elsewhere, is Hübner's meeting Palmerston at Paris in November of that year, in the course of which he said: "We are told, my Lord, that you don't like us," to which the reply was: "It is Austrian policy that I don't like. Your people at Vienna want a bad peace, a patched-up peace, instead of a good one": and a few days later Palmerston, dining with him, was still more outspoken. He said: "We are going to sign a treaty of alliance. If we lend ourselves to it, it will be with reluctance, and because we yield to the pressure put on us by the Emperor Napoleon. By an alliance, I mean your participation in the war. Well, you will never make war, and the sole result of this treaty will be strained relations between you and the Western Powers."

Palmerston's clear perception of the facts of the case is manifest. His judgment was no doubt assisted by the certain knowledge that Austrian statesmen could never sympathize with any policy of his, and that the apparent harmony of views between the three governments was intended solely to protect Austrian interests. The world in general is disposed to place more faith than is prudent in written alliances, but statesmen take them at their true value. I have often thought that they resemble marriage settlements, where each of the family solicitors engaged is chiefly concerned to secure the maximum of advantage for his own client. The negotiations for a defensive and offensive alliance between Prussia and Italy in 1866 afford an illustration. Austria gained her object, the evacuation of the Principalities, while England and France were left to carry on the war unaided.

There is no time to speak in detail of the important share of Hübner in the various negotiations that were carried on during the Crimean War, nor of the abortive discussions at Vienna in March, 1855, at which Lord John Russell was the First Plenipotentiary of England. He has been blamed for his failure on that occasion, but in my humble opinion, very unjustly. The real truth is that the terms proposed by the allies were in excess of what they were then justified in expecting Russia to accept.

After the evacuation of Sebastopol by the Russians and its occupation by the allies the negotiations were renewed, and the conditions previously rejected by Russia were accepted in January, 1856. The preliminaries of peace were signed at Vienna on February 1, and the definitive treaty at Paris on March 30. A fortnight later Austria, France and England entered into a treaty of alliance by which they declared that any infraction of the treaty of Paris would constitute a *casus belli*. Napoleon III, without asking the consent of his allies, communicated it to the Russian government. A few days later the congress separated.

From time to time during the earlier negotiations Hübner observed with concern that the relations between Austria and France manifested a tendency to become strained. Ill-feeling had been caused by the omission of the Emperor Francis-Joseph to send congratulations on the capture of Sebastopol, and when, in consequence of Hübner's pressing recommendation, instruc-

tions to offer them eventually arrived, Napoleon
refused to receive him for that purpose. His
anxiety lest a breach should occur was unceasing. During the congress he noted frequent
signs of a desire on the part of Napoleon to
conciliate Russia. Walewsky, who represented
France, habitually sided with the Russian pleni-
potentiaries, while the latter in turn spared no
effort to render themselves personally acceptable
to Napoleon. In the question of the new
frontier of Moldavia France ranged herself with
Russia against Austria and England. As an
instance of Napoleon's methods, the secret
arrangement made with Cavour that he should
vote with the Austrians and English so as to
form a majority against Walewski and Brunnow
is instructive. Buol on his part cherished
profound mistrust of French policy, and gave
vent to it in his official despatches and private
letters. Hübner exerted himself to smooth
matters over, not sparing flattery, and even
going so far as to congratulate Napoleon on the

skill with which he had broken up the league
formed against France during the first Revolution and maintained down to his own reign.
He was however unable to prevent the Italian
question being brought up for discussion, and
had to submit to its being mentioned in the
procès-verbal. Evidently the result of the
Congress was a defeat for Austria on this
point, though Hübner believed that Cavour had
obtained nothing of value. He might have
thought differently if he had known of Napoleon's
confidential utterances to the Italian statesman.

It has been the fashion of late years to
profess that the Crimean War was a political
mistake on the part of England, and, according
to a famous saying, that " we put our money on
the wrong horse." If it is meant by this that
the Western Powers should have left Turkey to
stew in the gravy which Russian diplomacy had
concocted for her, one may venture to differ
from several eminent statesmen. Probably
Kinglake's opinion is more plausible, that the

deliverance of Turkey from the exorbitant pre-
tensions of Russia might have been attained by
steady combined pressure on the part of the
Four Powers, and by leaving the leading part to
Austria, whose interests were more immediately
involved. If in that way an end could have
been put to the *tête-à-tête* with Turkey so dear
to the Russian mind, the isolated action of
England and France would have been needless.
But looking to the invincible repugnance of
Austria to the use of force, which is testified
to repeatedly by Hübner, it may be doubted
whether the united efforts of all four Powers
would have influenced the mind of the Emperor
Nicholas, since diplomacy unsupported by a
firm resolve to appeal to arms in the last resort
is rarely effectual. The war waged by the allies
resulted in converting the existence and independence of Turkey into a question of general
interest to Europe and putting an end to the
Russian claim to predominance, and since, under
the circumstances, there was no other way of

achieving this object, it must be held that the war was justified by its results.

To every statesman and diplomatist acquainted with the past history of the Italian question it must have seemed evident that the ancient rivalry of Gaul and Teuton would revive at no great interval of time. To exercise in the peninsula at least as great an influence as Austria had long been a French dream, of which the natural consequence was an endeavour to expel her altogether. Napoleon I had succeeded for a while, but his downfall brought back the Austrian, stronger than ever. During the forty and odd years that had elapsed since the Congress of Vienna several incidents had shown that the tradition had not been abandoned. Louis-Philippe's government had defied Austria by the sudden occupation of Ancona. The Republic of 1848 had announced its intention of coming to the aid of the independent states of Italy against any Power that disputed their right to change their constitutions, and Louis-

Napoleon, as already mentioned, had with great difficulty been prevented from going to war after the Piedmontese defeat at Novara. He compensated himself with the occupation of Rome. Hübner had long believed that the Empire would sooner or later create difficulties for Austria. Two things seemed to point to this conclusion, firstly the memory of Napoleon's youthful escapade as a volunteer with the Romagna insurgents of 1830, and secondly, his unconquerable hostility to Austria. At the Congress of Paris he and Buol had taken a personal dislike to one another, which was intensified on his side by Austrian opposition to several schemes dear to his heart. Of these one was the union of Moldavia and Wallachia. As time went on the relations of the two Powers were strained almost to the breaking point. When Napoleon III in May, 1858, despatched two vessels of war into the Adriatic to afford moral support to Montenegro against Turkey, it was only the fortunate prudence of the French

Admiral that prevented a collision with the Austrian forces in Dalmatia. Towards the end of the same year, when a revolt in Servia forced Karageorgevitch to take refuge with the Turkish garrison at Belgrade, and the insurgents threatened to attack the fortress, the Austrian government instructed the officer in command at Semlin to come to the aid of the Turks, if requested. A peremptory message was at once sent from Paris that if Austrian troops entered Servia it would be regarded as a breach of the Treaty of Paris, and Buol was forced to countermand the order. Hübner's was indeed no easy task. Over and over again he had to lament the acerbity of Buol's language, and once went so far as to inform the Emperor Francis-Joseph that it would be impossible to preserve friendly relations unless a change for the better took place in his chief's diplomatic manner.

During the year 1857, in spite of signs of coldness on the part of Napoleon he believed himself to have succeeded in exorcising the spectre, and that the danger was no longer imminent. He was not aware that so far back as November, 1855, when Victor Emmanuel paid a visit to Paris, the Emperor had said to Cavour: "Write confidentially to Walewski whatever you think I can do for Italy and Piedmont," though he knew of the proposal made to Austria, and rejected by her, that she should receive the Principalities in exchange for Lombardy and Venetia. Although he liked to fancy that Piedmont had gained nothing by being allowed to bring Italian affairs before the Congress of Paris, that was far from being the general opinion, and he too might have felt less comfortable if he had known that Napoleon had said to Cavour: "Be calm, I am certain that this peace will not last long," and that others were beginning to predict that the next war would be on behalf of Italy.

When Orsini in January, 1858, attempted Napoleon's assassination, Hübner, with his principal colleagues and the leading members of the French government, anticipated that the crime would lead him to break for good and all the ties which had bound him as a young man to the Carbonari. A letter of Orsini's to the Emperor, which was read at the trial contained the ominous words: "Remember that as long as Italy is not independent, the tranquillity of Europe and that of your Majesty will be but a chimera." In revising his journal forty-four years later Hübner added a note to the effect that "The Emperor of the French, placed on the pinnacle of greatness and accepted on a footing of equality by the heads of the old dynasties, had forgotten the engagements made in his youth with the directors of subterranean and unknown powers. Orsini's bombs recalled them to his memory. A ray of light must have suddenly illuminated his mind, and he must have comprehended that his former comrades never forget nor pardon, and that their implacable hatred is only appeased when the renegade re-enters the pale of the sect."

Certain scandalous Italian newspapers having glorified the act of Orsini, imperious instructions were sent to Turin to ask for their suppression. La Tour d'Auvergne in communicating them exaggerated their tone. Cavour refused to proceed otherwise than by legal measures against the offenders. It was desirable however to conciliate the Emperor, and Victor Emmanuel despatched his confidential aide-de-camp Della Rocca to Paris to offer explanations. He was at first coldly received, but being admitted to Napoleon's intimacy he found means of mollifying his resentment, and on his departure the Emperor entrusted him with a message to the King, promising in case of war with Austria to come to his aid with overwhelming forces. Cavour also was asked to correspond directly with him in order that they might come to an understanding. Then in July Cavour was invited to the famous interview at Plombières.

Not until after the lapse of many years did the nature of the colloquy that ensued come to be disclosed. Hübner was utterly unable to obtain any information. In August Walewski volunteered to repeat to him what the Emperor had said on the subject: which was that he entertained no hostility towards Austria—he sympathized with Italy, but would not go beyond the prescribed limits. Walewski explained this to mean that he would not go so far as to endanger peace, but the fact is that he had purposely been kept in the dark, in order that he might conceal the truth more effectually. What had passed can be read in Cavour's letter to the King of 24 July, 1858. The programme laid down by Napoleon and assented to by Cavour was in some respects fantastic. It was not eventually adhered to, but on the contrary was exceeded in a way that Napoleon had not contemplated. Cavour held all the trumps, but there was no reason to disclose them at once. He could afford to wait, and play them out as suited his game. The independence and unity of Italy were the stakes, and he won them.

Napoleon was drawn on by the irresistible logic of his own actions, and he had to look on while the Italians formed themselves into a considerable state, contrary to what had always been held to be the political interest of France.

At the end of November Hübner still believed Napoleon to be hesitating between opposite courses. Walewski on the 23rd assured the foreign ambassadors that there was no ground for alarm in the current reports of pretended preparations for war. The relations with all the Great Powers, he said, had never been more satisfactory, and if there existed any divergence of views between the French and Austrian governments, it was only on two or three minor diplomatic questions not of a character to endanger peace. It was true that the unofficial press, especially Prince Napoleon's organ, used language in contradiction with that of the Minister for Foreign Affairs, but Lord Cowley, who had recently paid a visit to

Compiègne, was of opinion that nothing was further from the Emperor's thoughts than to bring about complications in Italy. The *Moniteur* continued to rebuke the other papers for their attacks on Austria, and added: "The government of the Emperor consider it their duty to warn public opinion against the consequences of a discussion calculated to affect our relations with a Power in alliance with France."

Notwithstanding, on December 10, a secret treaty was signed with the Sardinian minister, embodying the arrangements made at Plombières, with a stipulation for the conclusion of a military convention. Walewski was now for the first time taken into his master's confidence. About the middle of the month Lord Cowley told Hübner that he continued to believe that the Emperor did not wish for war, though he might be dragged into it against his will, if complications arose in Italy. Napoleon's language about Austria was not favourable, and on several occasion he had said that things " could not go in this fashion." Prince Napoleon still continued his efforts to provoke war by means of the press, and Walewski to dispense tranquillizing assurances.

At length the bomb burst. On New Year's Day, at the reception of the diplomatic body, having replied to the Nuncio's congratulations with the words: "I hope the coming year will only cement our alliances for the happiness of nations and the peace of Europe," the Emperor said in a good-natured tone (*d'un ton de bonhomie*) to the Austrian ambassador: "I regret that our relations are not so good as I could wish, but I beg you to write to Vienna that my personal feelings towards the Emperor are always the same." Lord Cowley, says Hübner, saw in these words a proof of ill-humour, while his Russian and Prussian colleagues regarded them as a mere amplification of the reply to the Nuncio. The natural explanation seems to be that either they were provoked by the Belgrade incident already spoken of, which was not yet disposed of, or they were an unintentional revelation of what was at the bottom of the speaker's mind. They produced consternation throughout Europe. To still the alarm, Walewski attempted to explain that the Emperor had only intended to make a friendly remark, and the *Moniteur* published a *communiqué* to the effect that nothing in the diplomatic relations of the country authorized the fears to which certain alarming reports tended to give birth. The public instinct however was not deceived, and with justice, for at this very moment the military convention, eventually signed at Turin on January 18, was under discussion. Austria hurried reinforcements into Italy, explaining in Paris that this precaution was necessitated by the manœuvres of the anarchists, and had nothing to do with the Emperor's language on New Year's Day. At the same time Piedmont effected a concentration in the direction of the frontier. The marriage of Prince Napoleon with the Princess

Clotilde, part of the bargain between Napoleon and Cavour, took place on January 29. Five days earlier the *Moniteur* had contradicted the reports of a defensive and offensive alliance with Piedmont.

Efforts continued to be made to dispel the unfavourable impression that had been created. At a ball given at the Tuileries on 25 January both the Emperor and Empress were particularly gracious to Hübner. Walewski said he was more reassured as to the intentions of the Emperor, but hoped Austria would be prudent. The Emperor's speech at the opening of the Legislative Body on February 7 declared his hope that peace would not be broken. A short lull occurred, and pains were taken by persons supposed to be in the confidence of the Tuileries to persuade Hübner that the Emperor was coming round to a saner view of his position, partly, it was thought in consequence of the very decided language used by the parliamentary leaders in England. At the dinner given in honour of Prince Napoleon and his bride, the Emperor went out of his way to express surprise that his language on New Year's Day had been misunderstood. For the moment there was a faint hope that the war-cloud would pass away.

The endeavours of England to prevent a rupture were unceasing. Early in February the Queen wrote to Napoleon that she hoped he would prove to the world his "intention of adhering strictly to the faithful observation of treaties, of calming the apprehensions of Europe, and of restoring its confidence in the pacific policy of Your Majesty." In his reply dated ten days later he affirmed that he had told Piedmont during the previous summer that "his government could not encourage an aggressive line of conduct on her part, though she might rely on being vigorously backed, either if attacked by Austria, or if she became involved with that Power in a just and lawful war, but that these *pour-parlers* ended there."

4—3

He described the famous speech of January 1 as
"conciliatory words," and denied that he had
made any warlike preparations. The English
Cabinet then offered to send Lord Cowley on
a friendly mission to Vienna, and suggested
certain proposals for submission to Austria,
which were accepted with apparent goodwill
by Napoleon, all the more readily that he was
aware that the negotiation would lead to nothing. And so it proved, for convinced that
Napoleon was resolved on war, the Emperor
and Buol saw no advantage in making concessions. Before Lord Cowley could get back
to Paris, Russia, whether spontaneously or on
a hint from France, proposed a Congress of the
Great Powers for the purpose of considering
the means of preventing a conflict. France and
England accepted, and Austria agreed to go
into conference, provided that Piedmont first
disarmed, and to this condition she adhered
throughout. On her part she was ready to give
an undertaking not to attack Piedmont. There

were other minor points in dispute, but the real crux was disarmament, to which Piedmont declared her inability to accede, unless Austria disarmed also. For five weeks the ball was bandied about, until Austria, becoming weary of these futile negotiations and convinced that her antagonists were only manœuvring to gain time, announced her intention of taking the necessary steps to enforce disarmament on Piedmont.

Some fruitless attempts were still made by England to dissuade Austria from carrying out her threat, but on April 19 the summons to disarm was sent off from Vienna. It reached Turin on the 23rd, and on the 26th Cavour returned an answer tantamount to a refusal. The Austrian troops crossed the Ticino on the 29th. Even then England offered her mediation to Austria and France. The former accepted it, the latter declined. Napoleon's object had been attained, for had not the challenge come from the other side? That was what he had always insisted on as the condition of his coming to the aid of Piedmont. As he had foreseen, the English Cabinet laid the blame of the rupture on Austria. On May 2 the French Chargé d'Affaires at Vienna asked for his passports, and two days later Hübner departed from the capital where he had served his country faithfully, intelligently and with untiring diligence for the past ten years.

The foregoing narrative suggests several reflections. We have, in the first place, the almost tragic spectacle of a patriotic and devoted public servant compelled to contend for a bad cause— the cause of the continued domination of one people over another people which is striving for freedom. I presume there is not one Englishman to-day who does not rejoice in the thought that Italy, from being a mere "geographical expression," has come to be the name of an independent and self-governing nation, and that the dream of her great intellectual leaders of six centuries ago has at last been realized.

The second is, that the results of a successful war do not always—they may sometimes—fulfil the intentions and hopes of those that planned them. Nothing is more certain than that Napoleon III was far from desiring the unity of the Italian people. Yet that was the outcome of the war of 1859. Its more remote consequences were the war of 1866, which brought about the exclusion of Austria from Germany, the consolidation of North and South Germany under the leadership of Prussia, and the war of 1870 which ended in the downfall of his dynasty and the dethronement of France from her position of predominance in Europe.

And lastly, that governments can generally foresee the direction in which events are leading them, and that the utmost attainable by prudence and love of peace is the postponement of the evil day. The delay may be longer or shorter, for the precise moment of its termination cannot be predicted, owing to the incalculable effects of individual speech or action.

What in our ignorance we call an accident may
precipitate the catastrophe when we are hoping
that it is still far off.   But no confidence should
ever be placed in the most elaborate assurances
of pacific intentions, such as were lavished by
Napoleon and his Minister for Foreign Affairs.
It used to be said that history repeats itself, and
then again, that history does not repeat itself.
We may safely admit I suppose, that the
weather does not repeat itself; that to-day is
not a copy of yesterday, nor perhaps of the
same day of the same month last year, and so
on.   This want of uniformity does not however
prevent our expecting that an atmospheric de-
pression in the North Sea will produce a violent
storm on our eastern coasts, or that an anti-
cyclone approaching us from the south is probably the precursor of calm, fine and genial
weather.   Similar conditions are apt to produce
similar phenomena in politics as well as in
meteorology.   The study of history I under-
stand is an endeavour to trace the causes and

antecedents of political events in the past, with the object of forecasting the future—near or remote—in short, it may be regarded as resembling the science of meteorology. If it does not teach us what are the signs of approaching bad weather, it is difficult to see in what its practical utility consists.

www.ingramcontent.com/pod-product-compliance
Ingram Content Group UK Ltd.
Pitfield, Milton Keynes, MK11 3LW, UK
UKHW042149280225
455719UK00001B/203